IMAGES OF FRED DIBNAH

The images used in this publication are from the Keith Langston Collection unless otherwise stated.

**WHARNCLIFFE
TRANSPORT**

First published in Great Britain in 2012 by
WHARNCLIFFE TRANSPORT
An imprint of
Pen & Sword Books Ltd
47 Church Street
Barnsley
South Yorkshire
S70 2AS

ISBN 978-1-84563-162-8

The images used in this publication are from the Keith Langston Collection unless otherwise stated.

Typeset by Concept, Huddersfield, West Yorkshire.
Printed and bound in India by Replika Press Pvt. Ltd.

Pen & Sword Books Ltd incorporates the imprints of Pen & Sword Aviation,
Pen & Sword Family History, Pen & Sword Maritime, Pen & Sword Military,
Pen & Sword Discovery, Wharncliffe Local History, Wharncliffe True Crime,
Wharncliffe Transport, Pen & Sword Select, Pen & Sword Military Classics,
Leo Cooper, The Praetorian Press, Remember When, Seaforth Publishing and
Frontline Publishing.

For a complete list of Pen & Sword titles please contact
PEN & SWORD BOOKS LIMITED
47 Church Street, Barnsley, South Yorkshire, S70 2AS, England
E-mail: enquiries@pen-and-sword.co.uk
Website: www.pen-and-sword.co.uk

Introduction

Fred Dibnah – A Great Briton

The writer was fortunate to have known Fred and been able to observe up close the great man at work entertaining the British public with whom he forged a great and lasting affinity. Not that he would have called what he did work, Fred simply loved life, meeting people, talking to and interacting with them. A great many people will claim that Fred was their friend and they will all be right, in their own special way.

You didn't just meet with Fred, you were instinctively drawn close to him, his larger than life personality was truly infectious and his communication skills second to none. Fred had the uncanny and somewhat unique knack of talking through a TV camera so that the viewer actually felt a personal contact with him. Although a great traditionalist and a lover of all things Victorian, Fred Dibnah was what I believe the modern media people would call 'a natural', microphones and TV cameras did not faze him one bit. So enthusiastic for the subject matter in hand was he that in truth his eyes saw past the recording equipment, as if he was talking directly to you, his audience!

Proof of his many successes is fortunately preserved in tangible artefacts, on film and in the written word. His official recognition was highlighted by the award of his British Empire Medal (MBE) which deservedly came in 2004, having earlier been accorded the tribute of receiving not one, but two honorary degrees. But moving away from the public side of his life let us not forget that first and foremost, Fred was very much a family man.

Born like a great many of his admirers, in humble circumstances he was brought up to appreciate the values of companionship, honesty and the satisfaction which could be gained from a job well done. He was a greatly loved human being, and he left his unique mark upon the world he lived in, and accordingly it is a better place for his having been there.

Fred was born in Bolton, Lancashire, on 28 April 1938, and it was a town of which he grew to be fiercely proud – so much so that Fred never really took to the idea of Bolton being referred to as a part of Greater Manchester and would proclaim vociferously when hearing it referred to as such, 'It's Lancashire, Bolton in Lancashire!'

Fred seen at the top of the boiler house chimney at Barrow Bridge Mill, Bolton. He was about to fix the lightning conductor into position. (*Simon Warner*)

The man from the Telly! Fred's first meeting with Alistair Macdonald. (*Alistair Macdonald Collection*)

The terraced streets, canals and industrial landscapes of that fine town were to Fred places of high adventure. Tall smoking chimneys, steam trains thundering past near to the family home and a country recovering from the most horrific war ever visited upon mankind, were all important factors which collectively shaped the life of a person who was to arguably become one of the most interesting men ever to live and work in twentieth-century Britain.

Many have commented that Fred would have been good at whatever he chose to do and he certainly was a top notch steeplejack whose skills were much sought after by mill owners and industrialists. No doubt because of his successful television career Fred will more likely be remembered for knocking down chimneys in his own inimitable way, not for maintaining them to good order. Fred also had a real affinity with churches, well more accurately church (and for that matter town hall) towers.

One of Fred's many profound observations was that if you got it wrong steeplejacking there was a very good chance that you would later be spending 'half a day out with the undertaker'.

He never got it wrong. An interesting anecdote concerns his good friend ex-BBC TV reporter Alistair Macdonald, the man credited with first bringing Fred to our TV screens.

The story goes that during the filming of a 1980s news item the intrepid Alistair climbed with Fred. After the programme had aired some alarmed BBC suits (as Fred called them) asked Fred and Alistair to explain what they had been doing climbing without safety ropes, hard hats and the likes? You will have to imagine Fred's answer to those charges! It was said that thereafter (and until very recent times) that footage was used by the BBC Health and Safety bods to illustrate what not to do whilst filming on location!

In his inimitable way Fred Dibnah became 'the communicator' with his rich Lancashire tones serving to enrich his natural storytelling ability. With the advent of television he found a vast audience with whom to share an understanding of the things that were important to him. He possibly

At home with the TV crew, Fred works away on the engine whilst the cameras roll.

This is a still from the TV film which got Fred and Alistair Macdonald a ticking off from the 'Health & Safety' boys at the BBC. (*Alistair Macdonald Collection*)

succeeded where hundreds of our own school teachers failed; he made us willingly learn about subjects that we may previously have had no interest in at all.

Various social commentators have strived to analyse and quantify Fred's appeal and all in their own way come back to offer very similar explanations. He was they concluded 'ordinary'. Such a simple word! According to the dictionary it is used to denote that which is undistinguished, not remarkable and perhaps commonplace. But dear old Fred was none of those things; in fact he was the absolute opposite of them all. He was distinguished, very remarkable and definitely not a person who could ever be called commonplace. And yet for all that he was like us all and in that sense ordinary, he was simply one of us!

The popularity of his many television programmes are perchance, in addition to the obvious 'Fred Factor', testimony to the wide appeal of their content. For although some folks will say that they preferred this item to that (maybe because of their personal identification with the particular subject matter) they will also proudly tell you that they enjoyed them all equally.

This observer has a theory which I am sure is shared by others and it is that Fred's TV programmes are for a big cross-section of his audience a 'comfort zone'. They create in the watcher feelings of a warm and incredibly humanistic 'harbour' full of good values and solid logic in which we are invited to feel sheltered by and even allowed to wallow in. Nostalgia is never a bad thing in these frenetic times and Fred during his life, and fortunately now afterwards through the wonders of electronic wizardry, makes it something which we can still indulge ourselves with.

Dr Fred Dibnah MBE sadly died on 6 November 2004 after fighting a brave three-year battle with cancer.

Fred is survived by his brother Graham, his widow Sheila and ex wives Alison and Sue. He was the proud father of five natural children, to Alison there are daughters Jane, Lorna and Caroline and to Sue there are sons Jack and Roger. With Sheila his last wife, Fred took on the mantle of stepfather to her son Nathan.

After Fred's death I chose to describe him in print as 'A Great Briton'. Few if any would disagree. This is a collection of my favourite images from the many taken during the summer of 2004, plus a sprinkling of other appropriate Fred pictures for good measure. Enjoy in memory of Fred.

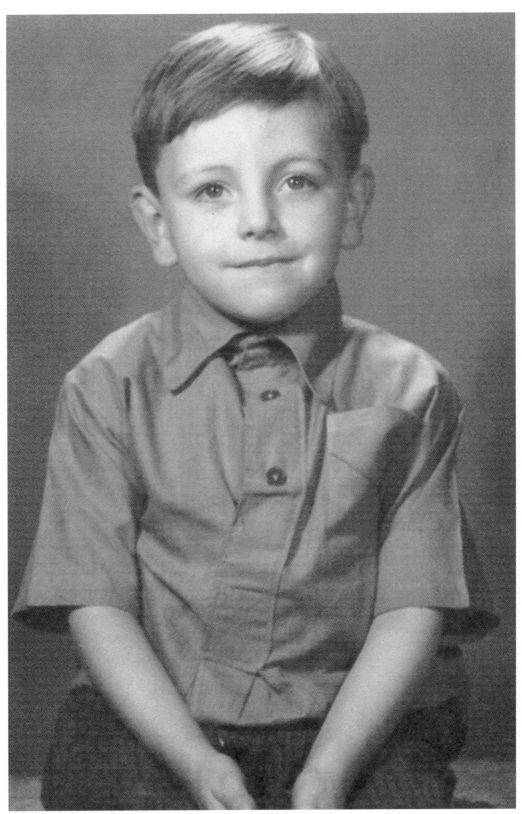

Fred the schoolboy.

Fred the soldier.

Dr Fred Dibnah after receiving his honorary doctorate from the University of Birmingham.

Alf Molyneux with Fred.

The Summer of 2004 – Fred's last TV project!

The Concept

The idea, for what sadly turned out to be Fred's last TV series, came mainly from his own desire to visit as many companies and individuals whose present day activities reflected the industrial advances which led to the development of steam machinery in general and his Aveling & Porter KND 4hp roller and motor tractor in particular. The 'convertible' had been an ongoing restoration project for Fred since he first purchased the machine in the mid 1970s.

The Crew

The series of programmes made by the production company 'The View from the North' was first broadcast on BBC2 in the spring and early summer of 2005. The senior members of the production team had all previously worked with Fred which led to a cohesive work plan and made the naturally difficult task of location filming easier to achieve.

Then producer and director of the series was David Hall and the production manager was Kathryn Hall and she in turn was assisted by Kate Siney. The majority of the camera work was in the capable hands of Rob Taylor and the regular soundman was Nigel Chatters. Jon Doyle also directed some of the location shoots and assisted on others, whilst Steve Shone and Steve Parry took care of the editing.

The Cast

In addition to Fred, his two pals, who are both ex coalmine workers, toured the country with him. Alf Molyneux and Jimmy Crooks had both worked on the restoration of the Aveling convertible and were also involved with the construction of the 'Pit Head Gear'. It has to be said that a great many of Fred's friends helped with the aforementioned projects. They are rightly due thanks and can be sure that Fred appreciated their constant help and support, but they are, of course, too numerous to mention individually.

Alf first became involved with Fred following a visit he and Jimmy had made to the site of Wet Earth Colliery in the Clifton area of Manchester.

Fred and his long standing friend Ian Thompson are seen working on the Aveling & Porter convertible steam tractor prior to its first outing after restoration.

Filming under way, crew members look on as producer/director David Hall talks to Fred as they set up for the next shot, the sound man is using the opportunity to make a test.

After retiring from their jobs as colliery over-men they pursued an interest in the history of that industry. Wet Earth Colliery is of national and international importance primarily due to the activities of James Brindley, the eminent engineer. Brindley's solution to water problems at the colliery remains unique in the annals of coalmining history.

Whilst at Wet Earth they bumped into Alan Davies who was then the curator of the now closed Salford Mining Museum. To further their acquaintance Alf arranged to meet up with Mr Davies later at a local public house. During that meeting another of 'the gang' Bill Richards introduced Alf to Fred Dibnah and the two men got around to talking about mining. Alf's interests were really roused when the subject of Fred's Pit Head Gear was discussed.

Fred asked him to call by and have a look at the scheme. He did, and in turn he recruited Jimmy, Alan Davies and several others to help in the digging of the pit. As Alf tells it, that was the start, and the rest is history. The

The 'Three Amigos' deep in conversation about a disused pit head which they had just visited in Nottinghamshire, left to right Jimmy Crooks, Fred, Alf Molyneux.

relationship which developed between the three men during filming, was fantastic and that clearly showed in the resultant programmes. Fred's infectious personality found the perfect soul mate in 'stoic' Alf, whose subtle sense of humour kept the whole crew constantly amused. Jimmy was the quiet man of the group and maybe that was a good thing, given that on a good day both of the others could talk for England! The on going saga of who pays for the tea and wads was always entertaining, and Alf still insists that Fred is related to royalty, as like them he rarely seemed to carry any money! A real bonus for Fred was the fact that his sons, Jack and Roger, were able to join him for most of the filming and the uplifting effect that had on him as he bravely battled his debilitating terminal illness was gratifying to behold.

The Journey

The Passion of a Lifetime

The journey took Fred to ancient iron foundries, industrial sites and also little workshops where things are still made today just as they were over 100 years ago. Fred at the beginning of the tour demolished his last ever chimney at a textile mill near Oldham. The group were then filmed making preparations to embark on the 'Grand Tour' with the steam traction engine.

Collecting the Coal

Coal of course supplied the power for the UK tour but finding the right stuff was a problem as there were at that time no merchants adjacent to Fred's home who were in a position to supply bulk coal on the big day. Therefore an open cast mine near Wigan was visited. On the first run it was literally an uphill struggle as the engine ran out of steam just a few miles from home. Problems sorted, and the fuel loaded, the boys journeyed to Astley Green Colliery Museum. On arrival the trio took a look at Europe's largest steam winding engine and examined closely three discarded Lancashire boilers, the construction of which fascinated Fred.

Who pays for the tea, again? Alf insisted that Fred was related to royalty, as like them he rarely seemed to carry any money!

17

Before hitting the road the boys needed to first extricate the van from the yard which meant a stiff uphill climb with a couple of sharp turns at the end of it, and all with a previously untried traction engine. What's more the living van was parked the wrong way around so had to be towed backwards. Alf had the difficult task of steering the front wheels using a long section of steel bar, brute force and the odd curse!

Nearly there, and by that time Jimmy was giving Alf 'moral support' with the task in hand! Fred on the controls was stoically pressing on whilst declaring, 'Everything forward and trust in the Lord'.

So far so good! Now all that remained was to get the living van and engine facing the same way, engine road number TA 2436 almost ready to roll!

Fred needed no excuse to open up the regulator and give the 'newly born' convertible tractor a thrash down the road.

Job done, all hooked up and ready for the off, coaling up was the next part of the mission.

Having travelled to Wigan in order to collect coal for the 'Made in Britain' trip Fred and the team stopped off at the Astley Green Colliery Museum which is just a stone's throw away from the A580 East Lancashire Road at Astley Green. Fred then began the process of checking over the Aveling & Porter steam tractor following its first road trip.

As the old song says, 'you have to get out and get under!' In addition to Fred, Alf and Jimmy, volunteers from the Red Rose Steam Society together with visiting enginemen lent a land, and in doing so they turned the occasion into a very pleasant social event.

21

Off came the copper chimney top for polishing, a little job for Alf, quipped Fred!

The complexities of steam compounding and the Aveling's cylinder block were the topic of this intense conversation.

Fellow steam man Richard Fairhurst and Fred took the opportunity to discuss the merits of steam rollers as Richard had brought his Fowler road roller along to the 'party'. Fred's roller Betsy (then back home in the shed at Bolton) was made by the rival Aveling & Porter company. Note the chimney top, Alf was off looking for a tin of 'Brasso'.

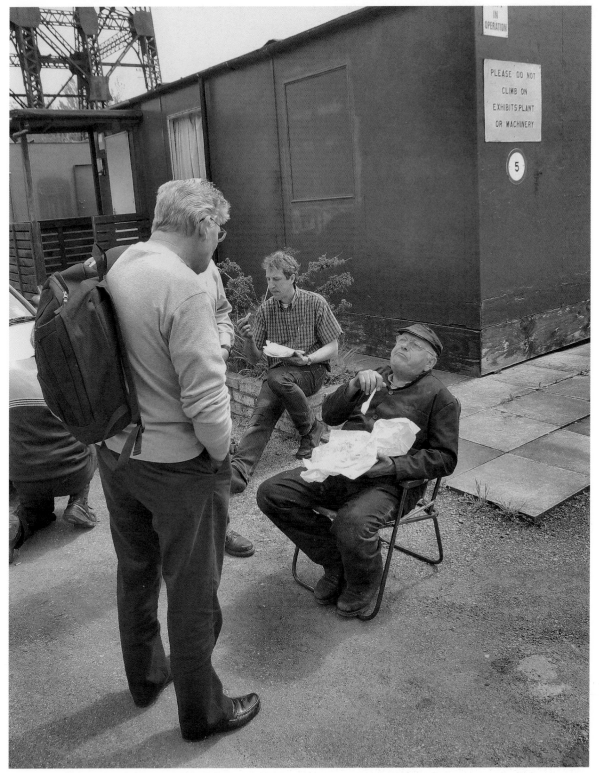

'We can talk steam all day but get your own chips!' There was a traditional chippie just outside the gates of Astley Colliery, the assembled steam enthusiasts made good use of it during the two day visit. As for Fred's chips it's a fair bet that Alf again got caught with his wallet open!

Fred and Richard still talking rollers, or are they? Sue (the author's wife) was there to take notes, but from studying this image and the look on Fred's face the subject under discussion could certainly be open to some interpretation!

Fred was well impressed with the superb preserved No. 1 Shaft Lattice Pit Head Gear at Astley; he is pictured giving the convertible tractor's smokebox door a final buff up in the shadow of the structure.

Astley Colliery

Coal was first recovered from the marsh land at Astley Green in the early nineteenth century, a 'modern' colliery at the site came into being circa 1900 and Astley Colliery was closed in April 1970. The impressive No. 1 Shaft (erected 1912) was intended principally for winding just over 8 tonnes of coal every two minutes from a depth of 801 metres, just short of 2,628 feet (there was also a No. 2 Shaft which was demolished). The Head Gear for the No. 2 Shaft is an impressive lattice steel riveted structure nearly 30 metres (approximately 98.5 feet) high. It was built by Head Wrightson of Stockton on Tees. The two winding pulleys are 6.4 metres (just short of 21 feet) in diameter and the whole structure weighs 122 tonnes. The Astley site represents the last remaining coalmine in the once vast Lancashire coalfields. It also houses the largest collection of mining locomotives in the UK and as such it is well worth a visit. (See www.agcm.org.uk)

The Source of the Iron

After leaving Lancashire the journey took them to the Lake District, an area not normally associated with industry, but where iron ore was once mined on a large scale in Cumbria. On the way, Fred stopped off to meet a friend,

Jack Dibnah, Dick Ransome and Fred give the Aveling Compound Convertible Steam Tractor a serious 'coat of looking over' during a stopover in the glorious Lake District.

Taking a newly restored steam engine 'on the road' meant making a few adjustments along the way; Jack, Fred and Jimmy Crooks were pictured during such an occasion. (*Jimmy Crooks Collection*)

Dick Ransome, a fellow steam enthusiast. Fred and company then enjoyed a sample of the beauty of the Lakes whilst taking a trip on board a steamboat owned by another friend and stalwart restorationist Roger Mallinson.

The next stop on the tour was Florence Mine at Egremont, the last deep iron ore mine in western Europe, which is still in commercial use. Fred took an underground tour during which he learned about the decline of the iron ore industry. Next the boys visited Workington Steel Works, at that time owned by Corus Rail; the site was once world-famous for making railway lines using west Cumbrian iron ore.

Castings

In the next part of the film, Fred and Alf travelled to Scotland where they were fascinated by the ingenuity of the 'Falkirk Wheel'. They also visited one of the few surviving traditional iron works left in the region. After stopping

Fred's love of all thinks Victorian was well known, accordingly a trip on Lake Windermere aboard his friend Roger Mallinson's restored period steam boat *Shamrock* was a real highlight. Roger (appropriately attired in striped blazer and straw boater) seems to be attracting the attention of his wonderful dog Whappet who listens intently, meanwhile Alf Molyneux 'played mother' as it was time for a brew! *(Roger Mallinson Collection)*

at the Bo'ness and Kinneil preserved railway for a few adjustments to the traction engine they travelled on to Queensferry. The steam roller then became the first such vehicle to cross the Forth Road Bridge under its own power.

Water and Boilers

Crossing the border back into England Fred visited Ryhope water pumping station in Sunderland, a facility that ceased working in 1967, after 100 years of service. Whilst in the north east they travelled across the Middlesbrough transporter bridge whilst taking a close look at the way it works. Israel

Newton's boiler works in Bradford was the next point of call. Fred considered that a real treat and remarked that the company 'still carried out boiler making the traditional way, by using rivets'.

The Road to Steel City

Another of Fred's ambitions was to drive a traction engine over the M62 motorway via the imposing Scammonden Bridge, and the opportunity to do so was taken on the way to visit Sheffield. Whilst in 'steel city' the friends took a tour around a forge and watched 'crucible steel' being made at the Abbeydale Industrial Hamlet.

Mechanics and Riveters

Whilst in Yorkshire, Fred and Alf stopped off at Andy Thornton's, a company who make beautiful ornate carvings and Victorian style wares. Fred tried his hand at carving and then watched a traditional 'ornate glass' cutter at work. On leaving the factory they had fun scaring a few small children with the steam whistle as they 'roaded off' to Worsborough near Sheffield, to have a go at making hot forged rivets in the traditional way.

The Midland Railway Centre

Travelling to Derbyshire they visited the Midland Railway Centre and toured the workshops in which railway locomotives were being restored and repaired. Fred was delighted to see a hydraulic riveter in action, especially as it was powered by an old Morris Minor car engine! Thereafter followed a visit to see more friends at Howard Brothers in Matlock, where a steam driven galloper, which had been destroyed by fire, was being lovingly rebuilt (now completed and often to be seen at steam events).

The centre operates standard and narrow gauge railways with preserved steam and diesel locomotives. The centre's Swanwick Junction Complex has a museum focused on the Midland Railway and highlights Midland Railway buildings in addition to housing a large collection of steam and diesel locomotives. At Butterley the MRC houses the Princess Royal Class Locomotive Trust Co. Ltd and that organisation are the custodians of several iconic steam locomotives including ex-LMS Pacifics No. 6233 DUCHESS OF SUTHERLAND and No. 46203 PRINCESS MARGARET ROSE. (See www.prclt.co.uk)

Pattern Making

Fred visited David Ragsdale a skilled pattern maker, who also owns six steam engines. David showed Fred around his traditionally configured workshops and foundry. Steam enthusiasts are renowned for their resourcefulness and a good illustration of that fact is Tom Nuttall a man who runs a garden

Camera rolled as the three mates and the engine arrived at the Midland Railway Centre, Butterley.

During the summer 2004 visit the British weather was up to its usual tricks, with intermittent rain and grey skies prevailing. However the team really enjoyed their visit to the Midland Railway Centre and took full advantage of an invitation to tour the steam railway engineering department's workshops, after first proudly showing off the Aveling & Porter convertible steam tractor.

Fred visited the boiler shop and he was particularly interested in their riveting equipment as he had made a similar machine for use at his own workshop, Jimmy looks on. The work piece is a locomotive boiler tube plate.

Fred with a group of kindred souls, steam engineers at the Midland Railway Centre, and of course those impressive dogs!

All smiles, Fred loved the working atmosphere of engineering workshops, he is seen at the MRC with an under restoration steam locomotive firebox and boiler.

centre and museum powered completely by steam, a 'set-up' that greatly impressed Fred.

Whilst in Derbyshire the team took a trip to Ashbourne and visited a traditional clockmaker. The whole workshop was belt driven, just like Fred's, and it has been a family business since 1826. Fred marvelled at the skills and techniques involved in the delicate processes carried out by the artisans.

Engines at Work

Fred met up with a few old friends at the North Staffs & Cheshire Traction Engine Club during a visit to their Klondyke base at Draycott in the Clay, Staffordshire. During the day a tree was felled using a steam tractor and steam driven wood cutting was demonstrated. In an additional display the art of 'scarifying' using a restored road roller was shown. All the clubs' engines were in steam so Fred was naturally in his element, chatting to kindred souls and later enjoying a pint or two! Whilst still in Staffordshire a visit to meet Len Crane at Bratch Pumping Station was undertaken. Len has spent the last six years restoring a huge triple expansion engine that was once used to pump water around the county.

The 'Bolton Boys' arriving at Klondyke Mill, the Staffordshire HQ of the North Staffs & Cheshire Traction Engine Club, Fred and Alf on the engine whilst Jimmy is on the steps of the living van with young Jack.

The Klondyke people had 'fired up' several engines especially for the occasion and Fred lost no time discussing the finer points of steam traction with NS&CTEC chairman Phil Jeffs and other members of the North Staffs & Cheshire Traction Engine Club.

Klondyke Mill – North Staffs & Cheshire Traction Engine Club

This long established and highly successful club have a permanent HQ, show ground, workshops and preservation centre just to the north of Draycott in the Clay village, Staffordshire which is situated just off the A515 Ashbourne to Barton-under-Needwood road. During the year several steam traction and special interest events are held at the centre. (See www.nsctec.co.uk)

Severn Valley Railway (SVR)

Once again steam railways beckoned and this time the team visited the Severn Valley Railway at Bridgenorth, Shropshire where Fred chatted with the train crews and toured the engineering workshops, but only after sampling the delightful 'bacon butties' in the station buffet. The historic town is built on two levels and being anxious to see the sights the crew took the 'convertible' for an extended trundle around the area.

If a point's worth making it's worth making well. You tell 'em Fred!

Time for a pint, the film company had kindly provided a barrel of real ale; Alf was pleased as it meant that on this occasion he didn't have to 'get his hand down!'

Good weather, good company, plenty of steam and a pint, Fred certainly enjoyed the occasion. Jack and Jimmy are looking after the ale and the living van steps etc. formed a makeshift bar.

During the filming at Klondyke Mill steam driven wood cutting was demonstrated, in this image Fred talks to the camera.

The boys arrive in Low Town, Bridgnorth, Shropshire and head for the railway station which is home to the main workshops of the famous Severn Valley Railway (SVR).

40

Once parked up at the railway, and gathered in front of the steam railway engine shed, producer David Hall, Fred and a couple of the SVR boys met to discuss the day's filming. Note that Fred has just observed that it 'looks like rain again' as you may expect there was also a small expletive in that observation!

After setting up for the day's filming and whilst dodging a summer shower Fred recalled that someone promised him a traditional bacon butty, and so the boys retired to the welcoming Bridgnorth station buffet. Much to the amusement of the onlookers Alf sat tight and asked the inevitable question 'who's paying?' Then adding that he had forgot his plastic card. Red letter day for Alf, Fred paid.

Steam men are steam men whether on the road or on the railway metals. Fred chatted to an SVR driver who then produced his note book which he asked Fred to sign.

Fred met several of the SVR engineers, who not only keep the steam locomotive fleet running but also helped to restore and rebuilt other engines, here he is seen chatting to a couple of Bridgnorth works guys about the merits of Great Western Railway engines beside locomotive No. 7802 BRADLEY MANOR.

Another break in filming at the SVR, no prizes for guessing who is again charged with polishing the Aveling & Porter engine's copper chimney top! With Fred, looking on is Alan Atkinson, a long standing friend and his regular low loader driver. Of course to facilitate filming the traction engine and living van had a little help getting around the UK! In fact whilst others slept Alan was often on the road in order to position the engine and van close to the next filming location.

Fred chats to his producer on the platform at Bridgnorth station, looking on is a gentleman from the blunt end of the country (south west), an ardent admirer of Fred's who was pleasantly surprised to meet up with him.

End of the day's filming at the SVR and Fred claims his reward, a much deserved pint of the 'Black Stuff'. The interesting looking walking stick belonged to the gentleman from the south west and it is apparently known as a 'wishing stick'.

After filming the boys decided to take the engine for a trip around Bridgnorth Low Town, and that meant crossing the mighty River Severn, this is the outward trip as the low loader was parked on the station approach. The area is well used to steam and smoke from the SVR but perhaps not from road vehicles!

Having travelled around Low Town the boys then re-crossed the river and headed for the station approach. Fred and Alf are on the engine with Jack on the living van steps and film maker David Hall shooting scenes from the door of the van.

For four decades, the Severn Valley Railway has graduated from relative obscurity to a prominent position in British railway preservation. The SVR is a full-size standard-gauge railway line running regular steam-hauled passenger trains for the benefit of visitors and enthusiasts alike between Kidderminster in Worcestershire and Bridgnorth in Shropshire, a distance of 16 miles. The journey is full of interest, for the route follows closely the meandering course of the River Severn which is set in magical countryside. The railway is mostly run by willing volunteers assisted by a small contingent of experienced professional staff. The SVR is considered by many to be Britain's premier preserved railway; accordingly the regular gala events and special themed weekends are well attended. (See www.svr.co.uk)

Chains and Copper

After leaving Bridgnorth, Fred, Alf and Jimmy visited the Black Country Living Museum at Dudley in an effort to learn about the mining history of the area. The Museum, which deals specifically with the history of an area which was of course at the heart of industrial England, was always a favourite location of Fred's. Its popularity may have been enhanced in his view by the attraction on site of a traditional 'chippie', a facility which the crew again took full advantage of.

Leaving the English Midlands the grand tour then moved to North Wales thus giving Fred the opportunity to drive the convertible though some stunning scenery. The old copper workings at Parys Mountain in Anglesey were visited on a grey drizzly day which added to the eerie atmosphere of the site which supplied the majority of the world's copper in the 1780s and continued to be a major player in the industry for 100 years. Whilst in Wales another railway visit was undertaken, this time the narrow gauge Ffestiniog Tourist Railway was the chosen location.

The Llanberis Pass

Situated in Snowdonia the pass carries the A4086 main road from the south east over Pen-y-Pass between the mountain ranges of Glyderau and Snowdon massif. The Welsh name is Bwlch Llanberis and an alternative English name is Pass of Llanberis. The height of the summit of the pass is 395 metres (approximately 1,296 feet) above sea level. If you have ever seen the comedy film 'Carry on Up the Khyber' you have seen the Llanberis Pass, as the area was famously the location for the making of that 1968 film.

The pass and surrounding area, in addition to being the start point of the famous Pyg Track, which allows walkers access to the summit of Snowdon (Welsh: *Yr Wyddfa*), is equally popular with walkers, climbers, abseilers in particular and tourists in general. Worthy of note on the roadside of the pass

Having travelled in advance of the film crew low loader man Alan Atkinson had already got the engine lit up and parked ready for unloading (albeit in the Sherpa bus stop at the top of the Llanberis Pass). Fred gives his beloved Aveling & Porter steam tractor a good coat of looking over prior to taking to the road.

Fred gets to work with the polishing rag before travelling down the Llanberis Pass.

Final preparations, the steam tractor's water tanks have just been filled courtesy of a tap in the 'Gentleman's Convenience', note the hose pipe at the rear of the engine which was craftily threaded through the window frame. Now I wonder who carried out that surreptitious move?

Triumphantly the boys head down the Llanberis Pass. As per usual Fred is controlling (driving) the steam engine and Alf is doing the steering, Fred's sons are on the living van steps and his youngest lad Roger can be seen sporting dad's topper!

are the Cromlech Boulders, which were fortunately saved from destruction in a 1973 road widening scheme after a successful six year protest by local people, climbers, historians, conservationists and geologists. The region is often rightly referred to as 'an area of outstanding natural beauty'. (See also www.llanberis.com)

Parys Mountain – Anglesey Copper Mines

This is a truly amazing part of north Wales which is closely connected with the history of copper production in the UK, and at one period in history the Anglesey Copper Mines' area was a major supplier of copper ore and products to a worldwide market. The production reached its peak around 1790–1800 when over 1,200 workers were employed recovering and partly processing copper in the immediate area, that activity in turn led to the rapid development of the nearby dock known as Amlwch Port.

But the history of mineral mining at Parys Mountain goes back much further in fact to Bronze Age and Roman times; fascinatingly a modern day mining company is still carrying out exploration in the area. Who knows the mountain could once again become an important player on the world ore markets?

Heading up towards 'Parys Mountain' on Anglesey and even on the misty wet day which greeted the crew the stark beauty and absolute eeriness of the place held a magnetic fascination. As Alf keeps his eyes firmly on the road ahead, Fred and film crew production assistant Kate Siney were obviously enthralled with the view of the valley below them and the surrounding landscape.

The boys have a good laugh at another's expense; in walking backwards to take pictures of their arrival at the Parys Mountain location this hapless photographer fell backwards into a very prickly and soaking wet gorse bush!

As the boys drove further up and into the once busy copper mining area the sheer enormity of the place became apparent.

The moonscape like vista which now dominates the mountainside on which the historically important mining site once stood is well worth a visit. Even TV time traveller Dr Who has visited; location filming for the popular series has taken place on Parys Mountain!

You can reach the history trail for Parys Mountain by leaving the town of Amlwch (also known as the Ancient Copper Town) going eastward along the A5025 and at the roundabout take the B5111 signposted for Llanerchymedd. (See also www.parysmountain.co.uk)

Welsh Slate and English Canals

After visiting the Welsh Slate Museum at Llanberis the team headed back to England but not before they had driven the Aveling down the famous Llanberis Pass, so that at the end of that journey Fred could try his hand at the art of slate splitting. The journey back to the north west of England included a visit to the fascinating Anderton Boat Lift in Cheshire where Fred enjoyed a ride down the Victorian lift followed by a canal boat trip.

'That's some hole in the ground', Fred gets his first view of the once active opencast copper workings at Parys Mountain, Anglesey, north Wales.

Anderton Boat Lift

The Anderton Boat Lift first opened on 26 July 1875 and the waterways' engineering wonder was built to carry cargo laden narrowboats between the Trent & Mersey Canal (at the top) and the River Weaver Navigation (at the bottom) in order to allow the transhipping of materials, which were originally salt and china clay. The lift was built to operate hydraulically but was converted to electrical power during 1908 and was ceremonially reopened as an electric boat lift in the July of that year.

Two picnic chairs, three Dibnahs! Jack, Roger and Fred squeeze onto the only available seats whilst waiting for the engine to be unloaded during a visit to the world famous Anderton Boat Lift, near Northwich in Cheshire.

The Boat Lift was always rated by Fred as being one of the greatest British engineering feats, accordingly he especially looked forward to his summer 2004 visit. Fred is pictured on the walkway of the lift and is standing at Trent & Mersey Canal level, whilst the River Weaver Navigation can be seen below and adjacent to the chemical works.

Given the go ahead by his British Waterways guide Fred sets of to explore the lift before filming commences. To the right can be seen the trip boat *Edwin C Clarke* aboard which visitors can experience the wonders of the boat lift for themselves.

Family conference up on the lift and it seems that Roger's question has the attention of not only his Dad, elder brother and a British Waterways official, but also Jon Doyle, the programme's assistant producer, who had just arrived in order to discuss the day's filming schedule with Fred.

Waterways engineer Gary Hughes shows Fred the inner working of the lift as the pair watch a boat lowered down to the river below.

TV cameraman Rob Taylor records the moment when Fred boarded a specially hired luxury narrowboat in order to take a trip down the lift.

The narrow boat enters the caisson full of water after which the rear gate will be closed allowing the caisson, boat and water to be hydraulically lowered to River Weaver Navigation below.

A magic moment for the holiday tripper aboard the other narrow boat in the caisson, as the lady suddenly recognised Fred and hurriedly produced pen and paper! Fred naturally obliged by signing her book as the boats took their downward journey.

The splendour of the magnificently restored Anderton Boat Lift can be appreciated in this image taken as the boat carrying Fred sailed free of the caisson and entered the River Weaver Navigation. It is easy to appreciate why the lift has justifiably earned the title 'Cathedral of the Waterways'.

Father and son enjoy a together moment during a break in filming, Fred and Jack at the Anderton Boat Lift.

After many years' service the boat lift was eventually closed to traffic in autumn 1983 after giving a century of service. Of course by that time canal freight was almost completely a thing of the past, following the expansion of road and rail traffic. But the waterways went on to become important leisure highways and in 1994 a move to reinstate the historically important lift began.

The lift was officially re-opened on 26 March 2002 after a publically supported restoration effort which took two years' hard work and an estimated £5.5 million to complete. The reinstated lift is once again hydraulically powered and stands as a tangible reminder of British engineering skills of the past, the iconic structure and its visitor centre are well worth a visit. (See also www.andertonboatlift.co.uk)

Engineering Workshops

Fred's appreciation of engineering workshops, especially those that use traditional methods, is well known and two companies whose components were used on the Aveling rebuild were therefore visited. They were the Budenberg Gauge Co., a German concern who first opened a Manchester depot in 1857, and Thomas Smith & Sons of Atherton who supplied Fred with his bolts, rivet blanks and threaded steel bar.

Engineering Excellence

The final part of the journey included another visit to a steam railway and this time the chosen location was the Great Central Railway at Loughborough. On this trip Fred got to drive a steam locomotive during a round trip on the preserved line.

After leaving the GCR the crew continued south as Fred had business in the capital! But first they visited The Crossness Pumping Station which was built by Sir Joseph Bazalgette as part of Victorian London's urgently needed main drainage scheme. First opened in April 1865, it houses four original rotative beam engines, the greatest collection of such engines in the world.

Great Central Railway

Voted number 12 on the list of the 50 greatest railway journeys in the world the Great Central Railway is the UK's only double track, main line heritage railway. It's the only place in the world where full size steam engines can be seen passing each other – just as it was when steam ruled the rails.

Trains run every weekend of the year, bank holidays and selected weekdays through the summer. The GCR also run many family themed events, including Bonfire Night, Wartime Weekend, Santa Specials and additionally special enthusiast gala events.

Fred, Alf and the boys took the Aveling & Porter convertible steam tractor along the streets of Atherton during the journey to the works of Thomas Smith & Sons, and all were enjoying the glorious July sunshine.

Appropriately named soundman Nigel Chatters prepares to get Fred wired for sound!

Fred proudly shows of his greatly deserved MBE during a 2004 visit to the Great Central (preserved) Railway. Unexpectedly fishing it out of his breast pocket he joked 'this 'ere cross goes well with my work gear and it means I outrank you lot!'

'You missed a bit Alf,' said Fred. Ex-coalminer Alf Molyneux and Fred were good mates and they are seen polishing up the Aveling & Porter tractor's brass chimney top ring, a ritual which was observed before every road run. Fred's admiration for steam traction was legendary and he loved working on steam conveyances or as he called it 'backstreet mechanic-ing'.

The TV work which came along in the 1980s, following an earlier filmed interview on BBC 'North West Tonight' from the top of Bolton Town Hall, which first brought Fred to the attention of the wider public, but we must not lose sight of the fact that he was first and foremost a highly skilled working steeplejack. Fred's handmade weather vanes were very treasured possessions and fit to grace any building.

Never one to shirk a challenge! Fred peddles a custom built floating cycle along a disused stretch of the Bolton & Bury Canal. The stunt was a part of promoting locally the idea of reopening the canal for leisure use. *(Bolton & Bury Canal Society)*

One of Fred's favourite examples of great British engineering triumphs was the Anderton Boat Lift, near Northwich, which famously connects the Trent & Mersey Canal at the top with the River Weaver Navigation in the valley below. Fred is seen whilst inspecting a luxury narrow boat on which he would later take a trip down the lift.

A smiling Fred enjoys the view from the top of Anderton Boat Lift a structure which has rightly been referred to as the 'Cathedral of the Waterways'. The lift was conceived and built by a group of enterprising Victorian engineers in order to convey narrow boats loaded with cargo between the two waterways, the main cargos carried being salt and china clay. It was first opened as a hydraulic lift in 1875 and later changed to electric power in 1908. The lift fell into disuse as canal freight traffic declined circa 1980, but later following a preservation struggle and then eventual restoration it was returned to use and reopened in March 2002 in the form of a modern hydraulic boat conveyance fit for the twenty-first century. A visit will serve to illustrate why Fred thought it was 'a Victorian edifice to be proud of, and one of the greatest engineering feats of that era'.

All that remains of a once tall Victorian era mill chimney is a smoking pile of bricks, where once stood a busy cotton mill which employed a large proportion of the local community will soon be a new housing estate. Such was Fred's love for those structures that he used a special method of toppling unwanted chimneys (and in some cases other tall structures). The use of explosives may be effective but in Fred's opinion such a violent end was not a fitting way to dispose of something which men had long ago laboured so hard to build. Fred's special method meant that each chimney toppled would at least have one last good smoke! This picture was taken on the occasion when Fred dropped his last chimney. It was Sunday, 9 May 2004, the location was the former Lion Mill at Royton.

Because of the TV programmes Fred's mine shaft, constructed on a slope in his back yard, became nationally famous. It was built with good reason as Fred rightly thought it important to show future generations how things used to be. Had he lived long enough to finish his 'pit head' project it would have had a working shaft complete with winding engine and cage connecting with a tunnel below. At the lower level railway lines with suitable coal mining trucks would have been put into place. In this 2003 image Fred is explaining the construction methods used with the help of his detailed working drawing, his living van in this instance serving as the engineer's site office.

Fred and Alf take to the streets of Bolton and pass close to the town centre taking the first ever combined road trip with the newly restored Aveling & Porter steam tractor and living van in the spring of 2004. Note the brewery chimney in the background similar to many Fred had worked on in the area and in fact throughout the country.

In 2004 Fred, Alf and the two young Dibnahs, Jack (left) and Roger (right), took the convertible steam tractor up into the old copper workings at Parys Mountain in Anglesey. You could be excused for thinking this was an autumn scene but in fact it was a very gloomy August day.

Fred, with a bevy of young passengers and Alf, at the wheel took his steam tractor onto the open road and travelled from his home in Bolton to the works of Thomas Smith & Co. at Atherton during the summer 2004 filming project.

Fred had his own unique way of explaining engineering matters in easy to understand terms, in this image he is seen in the back yard of his Bolton home whilst talking to camera.

Filming is about to get underway, Alf is chatting to a Thomas Smith & Sons employee whilst Fred smiles for the photographer!

Fred in full cry as the camera turns. Outside the previously sunny day had turned decidedly showery, well after all we were in the middle of an England summer! Alf appears preoccupied with the work piece in the furnace.

Fred and Jack discuss a modification which they needed to make to the firebox door of the convertible.

Learning the script at the GCR.

Resting between 'takes' at the Great Central Railway. Left to right: Roger, Fred, Alf Molyneux and Jimmy Crooks.

'Give us a go!' Fred persuades the duty locomotive driver at the Great Central Railway to let him have a go at driving the restored ex GCR '04/1' class 2-8-0 steam locomotive.

The engine crew welcome Fred onboard the footplate of their locomotive for a trip along the route of the restored railway.

Off we go, Fred has a firm grip of the locomotive's regulator. He had earlier told Alf 'there's no steering wheel on this!'

The Great Central Railway (GCR) 'Mess Room' and at bagging time Fred is entertaining the troops with another humorous anecdote, delivered in his own inimitable style!

Fred's 'Member of the British Empire' medal (MBE) gets an airing at the GCR, together with a wink and broad grin for the camera.

71

Oops! . . . the brew can takes a tumble.

Fred received his justly deserved MBE from HM Queen Elizabeth II.

The Dibnah boys seen in London before putting on their dress suits for the trip to the Palace, note the Dibnah 'ten to two' or if you prefer 'ten past ten' stance!

Fred dressed for action, boots and all!

Fred Dibnah or Fred Astaire? A little jig seemed appropriate as Fred set off for the Palace.

Filming in London. Fred talks to the camera in his 'palace suit' Picture taken from the 'wings'.

During Fred's London visit the Aveling & Porter steam tractor lodged at Wellington Barracks alongside Birdcage Walk. At that time the Irish Guards were in residence and Fred took the chance to recant some of his national service experiences with the officer in charge.

'Let's head for town.' Fred turns the engine and van around on the parade ground at Wellington Barracks.

Houses of Parliament again, and its still raining.

Parked in Whitehall. '*Veni, Vidi, Veci*' said Fred, or something like that anyway!

'Let's go this way.' Alf steers the engine past the Churchill statue and around into Parliament Square, a truly remarkable scene, young Roger (sat on the back of the engine) was enthralled. As for the London public they found it hard to believe their own eyes!

'Keep going Alf, past the big clock.' In fact, the boys were so impressed that they actually went around the block again, much to the delight of what had become an appreciative crowd. The Dibnah boys loved every minute of it.

Having done Parliament Square, and after a quick out and back crossing of the Thames the boys then headed for Whitehall, well why not!

The engine has just passed the Cenotaph, note the cyclist who was about to overtake and then slowed to have a good look at the 'Northern Interlopers'.

Crossing the Thames with the famous St Thomas' Hospital in the background, and a red London bus close behind.

On Whitehall again and by this time Alf was concerned about the need to take water and wanted to look for a fire hydrant. Fred's look says 'over to you Pal' whilst Roger (sporting Dad's top hat) simply enjoys the moment. Those who have come out of their offices to watch the very 'un-London like scene' are more than a little bemused!

Heading up Birdcage Walk, with Fred and Jack on the engine, and a member of the film crew taking shots from inside the living van door.

London taxi drivers are rarely fazed by what they see in the capital during rush hour but the unusual sight of the engine complete with living van, whilst stopped on double yellow lines for a 'blow up', caused the driver and his passengers to stare in surprise.

84

The railway has won a number of awards including 'Independent Railway of the Year', a gold award for the East Midlands 'Best Visitor Experience' and is a quality assured visitor attraction as designated by Enjoy England. (See also www.gcrailway.co.uk)

The Trip to the Palace

The highlight of the 'Great Journey' was the visit to Buckingham Palace where Fred received his justly deserved MBE from HM Queen Elizabeth II. The honour was awarded for services to broadcasting and industrial heritage. The presentation of the 'Gong' was followed by an impromptu celebratory parade around the City of Westminster, an area used to a lot of hot air but not usually steam!

Whilst Fred and the boys would dearly have loved to 'steam' between locations the pressure of filming schedules prohibited them from doing so. In order to transport the engine and van around the country quickly the use of a low loader vehicle was essential. Fred's regular driver was Preston based contractor and friend Alan Atkinson seen in this image with the Dibnah boys whilst preparing the ensemble for the move back north after the London filming stint.

12.00 Noon, Tuesday, 16 November 2004 – Bolton Parish Church.

Epilogue

The plans for filming 'Made in Britain' included trips to the West Country, South Wales and the Forest of Dean but unfortunately Fred's rapidly-deteriorating health prohibited those plans being carried out. Whilst fighting cancer Fred's achievement in completing the huge amount of filming which he did, during the spring and summer of 2004, was nothing short of miraculous. His braveness in the circumstances was inspiring and as such was a credit to his strength of character and can be taken as a source of inspiration to us all.

Chimney Demolition Fred Dibnah style!

Born in pre-war Britain during 1938 Fred Dibnah was according to his mother always interested in his surroundings and in particular anything to do with climbing, or that which involved steam. As a small boy he loved to watch steeplejacks at work on the chimneys and tall buildings of his native Lancashire home town of Bolton. From his bedroom window he could see steam locomotives at work, and he would sit and watch them for hours.

Whilst watching those artisans he studied the way that they erected their ladders and built scaffolding no doubt formulating in his mind the way he would do the job when his time came. The time did of course arrive when like most people he needed to choose how to earn a living and support a family. It was to his love of climbing tall structures that he turned in order to be able to put bread upon the family table.

The traditional industries were starting to show signs of age and irreversibly the industrial Britain which Fred loved was undergoing changes, which for better or ill would irrevocably and completely reshape the nation. The demise of those traditional factories and indeed the redundancy of their very fabric was at first a good thing for Fred's growing enterprise. Factory chimneys, which for many years had been carefully built and then lovingly maintained, would now need to be demolished.

The well-built traditional boiler house chimneys were seen in Fred's eyes as structures of great beauty, and he often referred to them as such, each being the greatest compliment anyone could ever pay to the people who built them, he justifiably referred to those chimney builders as hard men. To simply destroy them with dynamite at the end of their useful lives did not appeal to Fred Dibnah, and anyway he reasoned that because of their location they would often need to be more carefully dismantled.

That special kind of demolition was achieved by what he once termed 'backards' construction. Having climbed the condemned chimney Fred then removed the bricks course by course and either dropped or lowered them safely to the ground. But there was another way which also got the job done, no explosive charge was employed but plenty of drama was created. This particular method Fred made all his own.

The sandwich! Note the sections of pit prop (with drilled holes) which are placed between short lengths of scaffolding plank and lastly the filling of scrap timber.

From the 1970s onwards Fred's fame as a toppler of chimneys (and tower type structures) became almost legendary. Using his tried and trusted method, Fred safely reduced many a once proud structure to rubble.

Fred's method was on the face of it simplicity itself, although of course the danger is very real, and only by applying the skills born of many years experience did Bolton's most popular son make it look so easy.

Having decided in which direction they want the redundant structure to fall the demolition gang first cleared an area a good bit larger than what would be the chimney's estimated 'lying down' size. It was then the turn of Fred and his small, but expert team, to take over.

Slots would be chiselled in the side of the chimney and bricks are removed from the opening making it roughly 3 feet high by 1½ feet wide or if you prefer two bricks wide by twelve bricks high, apology to those of a metric leaning Fred often measured with a fifty year old 'yard stick'. Two sections of scaffolding plank (approximately 8 inches wide) were then cut so that their length just exceeded the thickness of the brick layers in the chimney wall.

The next move was to insert the 'filling' in the scaffolding plank sandwich, a piece of wooden ex-telegraph pole or similar, which then takes on the role of a 'pit prop' and so holds up the bricks above it, (i.e. taking the place of those removed). Thereby after leaving a section of three bricks in width the exercise is repeated at a position further around the base of the chimney until the required number of slots and props were in place.

The bricks between the props would then be carefully removed so that the chimney, on the side of the chosen direction of the drop, is entirely supported by the newly inserted wooden supports. Thereafter a couple of holes were drilled through the width of each pit prop. The holes, according to Fred were put there as an aid to combustion, they allowed the flames to get inside the wood quicker.

The next essential ingredient to be added was the timber debris from the demolished buildings and selected sections of that were packed between the props from the bottom to the top of the 'letter box' styled slot. That done a huge bonfire of the remaining scrap wood was built against the side of the chimney, completely covering the props and the inserted wood. The next ingredient to be added was a few gallons of diesel fuel, until all the wood was well and truly soaked in the petroleum accelerant.

All that was then required in order to topple the chimney was a piece of wood approximately 2 inches in length and ⅛ inch in cross section. Providing the brimstone covering on one end of that piece of wood was nice and dry then the quick application of the laws governing friction would do the rest. As the resultant fire gets hold the supports burn away and Mr Isaac Newton's law would do the rest.

A bonfire of scrap wood was then built against the side of the chimney.

The next ingredient to be added was a few strategically placed gallons of diesel fuel.

When the appointed time approached, the VIPs and watchers were all moved to a safe distance. Fred would always pronounce how long each burn would last, often no less than twenty minutes and no more than twenty five. The match was struck and applied to a diesel soaked rag which was then placed into the bonfire. Within minutes the blaze would get a real hold, aided by the diesel oil. As if in a last proud act of defiance the chimney would begin to smoke profusely as the timber packed inside the structure ignited.

The sky turned black with smoke and the watching public downwind could be showered by the soot carried in what would be the great chimney's last gasp of breath. The huge crowd of spectators were always to a person enthralled, and often remained almost silent during the burn. As the fire roared onward and upward the black cloud turned to a hotter lighter colour and at that point the nearby watchers would take another step or two backwards.

Anytime now, 'don't miss it I can't put it back up!' says Fred.

Another one bites the dust, 'did you like that?'

Fred would explain that when the end of the chimney's stand is almost nigh he expected a brick or two to split, and the resultant rifle like retort would, he prophesied, be the signal which heralded the collapse of the stack.

He almost always told the press and TV cameramen to listen and look very attentively, as he said that he was not able to repeat the show should they fail to capture it on film!

The tell tale retort would be heard just prior to a huge split opened in the back of the chimney whilst at the same time sections of brick work would fall

away from the front (in the direction of the intended fall). In the twinkling of an eye, in fact during the duration of just ten frames of electronically exposed 35mm film, it was all over.

Within days the brick layers, joiners and other tradesmen would be starting to put up the new houses, removing forever another trace of our industrial past. As for the crowds they went on their way happy having been well entertained by what for most of them had been a once in a lifetime occasion.

A lady autograph hunter gets her man.

After Fred's fire had done its job, the laws of gravity took over at Park Mill, Oldham, in 1985.

Down she goes! A 150ft chimney at McKechnies Copper Smelting Works in Widnes bites the dust, March 1991.

Fred dropped his last chimney on Sunday, 9 May 2004 at Lion Mill Royton near Oldham. The young admirer has just collected Fred's autograph.

Fred's Mineshaft

It's doubtful if anyone else would first sink and then brick line a shaft and erect above it coalmine type pit head gear, complete with a working winding engine, in their own back yard. In 2003 Fred Dibnah did!

The pit head gear and shaft was located on a slope and when completed a short tunnel built at 90 degrees to the shaft (incorporating a light railway with authentic coalmine trucks) would exit at the bottom of the slope, alongside the river which bordered Fred's land. The structure would in every sense be a fully functional exhibit showing clearly the workings of a small coal mine.

The brick lined shaft seen when under construction.

Another of Fred's happy band – ex-miner Bill Richards seen with Fred and Alf after the pit head gear had been built in 2003.

The skillfully designed and built structure, said Fred, would be 'a lasting and tangible reminder of the once vast and highly productive Lancashire coalfield'.

Fred explaining the construction methods which he and his mates had used to create his very own mineshaft.

The authorities brought in experts to try and force Fred to fill in the shaft claiming that in digging it he had caused the sloping land to become unstable, and thus subject to slippage. But that official move backfired on them when 'their' expert actually found that in sinking and lining the shaft Fred had in reality made the slope much more stable!

Fred with the mineshaft, a project he would sadly not complete.

Fred examining the mineshaft in his back garden.

Fred talks to camera just prior to setting off on his round-Britain tour. 105

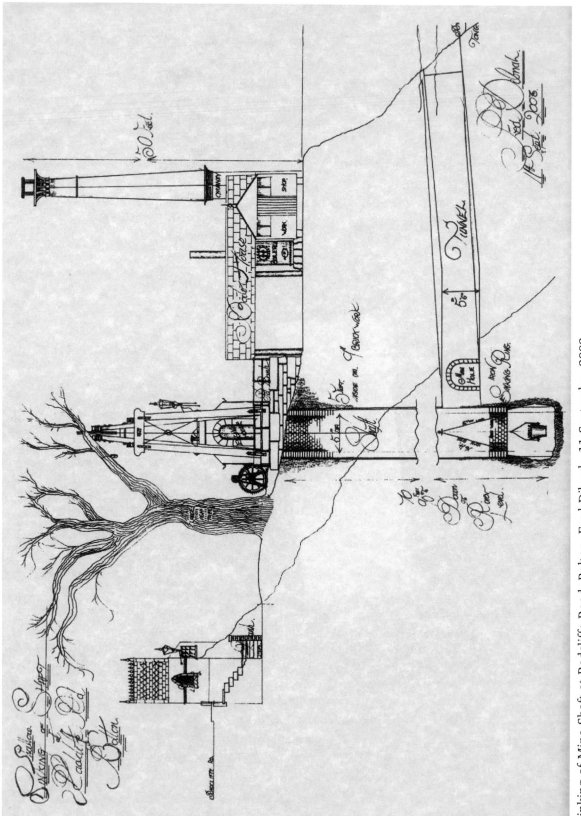

Sinking of Mine Shaft at Radcliffe Road, Bolton. Fred Dibnah, 11 September 2003.

The Eyes Have It

Following on from the tale of Fred, the BBC and Bolton Town Hall, there is another tale concerning derring do and matters of a civic nature that needs telling, although a delicate touch may be the order of the day.

The somewhat unusual anecdote was recounted for all our benefit by Bill Greenhalgh, with whom Mr Dibnah got into what have been described as 'a few scrapes', which I suspect is one of the biggest understatements of all time!

But back to Bolton's major civic edifice. The original town hall, of which Fred was fiercely proud, was opened on 5 June 1873 by HRH Albert, Prince of Wales. There was a hall in that fine building named in honour of the young prince but sadly, the original majestic building was ravaged by fire on 14 November 1981.

The conflagration reportedly started in the basement and destroyed the original Albert Hall but, as fortune would have it, the rest of the building was saved. The damaged section was later rebuilt as the new Albert Hall and Festival Hall, both of which are used for functions.

Fred having a quick fag while giving the job a coat of looking over.

There is more than a little irony where the creation of Bolton's town hall and the message in the town's motto is concerned.

The civic motto is 'Supera Moras' which literally translates as 'Overcome delays' but the time that lapsed between the original town hall proposal being submitted and the completion of the building was the thick end of seventy-seven years! However, as someone's granny in those parts is sure to have said at some time or other: 'There's nowt got with rushing – only babies!'

Bill Greenhalgh is known locally as a designer of buildings but it was also rumoured that he did get his hands dirty on occasions, and this is an account of one of those occurrences.

Fred carried out a fair bit of work at the town hall during the late 1970s including famously the

Bill Greenhalgh's superb water colour of Bolton town centre, showing the town hall with its cupola.

108

gilding of the globe, which first brought him to the attention of the BBC. He always said that the civic jobs were not big payers, more labours of love. One such labour was repairing the columns to the cupola (a small dome above the central roof).

The council, no doubt with one hand firmly on the purse strings, had asked Fred to repair/replace the pillars using glass fibre, a request made during a site meeting at altitude.

At that suggestion, Fred reportedly went ape and marked the council engineer's card in good style. He left the poor guy in no doubt that only 'proper' stone would do and that he – Fred Dibnah – would not put his name to what he said would be 'a right shoddy job using that new fangled fibre stuff!'

There was no more to be said. Doubtless the council guy saw discretion as the better part of valour and diplomatically climbed down to terra firma – but only after telling Fred to get the job done as he saw fit.

Having recruited Bill Greenhalgh to help him, Fred completely bamboozled his friend by first sending him to the scrapyard in search of an old washing machine.

Why, thought Bill, as he haggled with the scrapper over a couple of bob, did Fred want a bloody washing machine? On arrival back at the yard, Fred asked Bill if the one he had procured had a good motor?

Funnily enough the scrapyard man had said that it did, but that the pump was knackered. All was then made clear as the ever-ingenious Fred ripped the old Hotpoint apart, removed the motor and told Bill to dump the rest back with the scrapper, adding: 'There's enough crap around the yard as it is!'

Clear as mud? Well, of course not. Fred built a stone-cutting lathe and used the washing machine motor to drive it. Bill recalls that the stone was bought from a local firm, Bramhalls Monumental Masons, and a sample column was made. The pair took it to the powers-that be for approval, which was readily given, and the rest of the columns were made to the same pattern. Scaffold was erected on the town hall roof so work could commence.

Bill recalls that the job went well and, as always, Fred's work was of the highest standard. But for the colour of the new mortar, you had a job to tell the new from the originals, he declared.

During a smoke break they had been looking around the dome and noticed that what they first thought were little blobs of stone above their heads were, in fact, lions' heads cut into the stone. Fred was preoccupied with this for some time.

The last day of the job arrived.

'We had hauled all the last gear up to the scaffold including a new batch of mortar which we kept loose with water we had brought up with us,' said Bill. 'When we had finished we both lit up and stood back to look at out handiwork. "Champion", said Fred, and I have to say the columns really looked the business.'

It was then, Bill recalled, that Fred's face acquired a cheeky smirk as he gazed at the stone lions' heads above them.

'I am going to make them buggers see,' he declared, as he pointed to the carved lions. He then produced a handful of glass marbles like the ones kids play with from his pocket.

No sooner said than done – and up he went. His drill reamed out a socket in each of the lions' eyes.

The pair hadn't noticed the impending gloom and as they began to mortar the 'alleys' into their new homes, they became aware that the mix was getting too dry to work with.

Bill recalls what happened next.

'We realised that we would not be able to go down for water – a precarious round trip of about forty minutes – as by the time we got back it would be pitch black. A Victorian town hall roof is really no place to be after dark.

'There was nothing for it. Needs must when the devil drives, as they say.

'Having worked up there for four hours since our last break, we both, fortunately, had very full bladders. The strained best bitter worked perfectly in conjunction with the mortar!

'We finished the extra job, thus becoming immortalised in urine at the top of Bolton Town Hall.

'Not a lot of people know that!'

A Bronze for Fred

The date 29 April 2008 would have been the late Fred Dibnah's seventieth birthday. Although a modest man, Fred would have loved the memorial to his memory unveiled in Oxford Street, Bolton, on the anniversary of that occasion, especially with his five children looking proudly on.

But the significant bronze statue was only made possible by the generosity of his many admirers and friends. Thousands of people nationwide contributed to the fund set up by Bolton & District Civic Trust. On 6 November 2004, the day Fred was sadly taken from us, his long-standing friend, Bill Greenhalgh, vowed that the town of Bolton would have a suitable memorial to its famous son. Unbeknown to Bill, a lady journalist on the other side of town was having similar thoughts!

Fred's very proud children, seen after the unveiling ceremony. From left: Jayne, Lorna, Caroline, Jack and Roger.

The grandchildren get a day they'll remember: Christopher and Daniel (Jayne's), Isobel (Lorna's) and Jack (Caroline's).

Bill found a fellow traveller in the person of Brian Tetlow, chairman of the town's Civic Trust. The pair met with the local paper where deputy editor Lynn Ashwell told them of her ideas. 'Lots of people had statues in the towns where they were famous. Eric Morecambe's famous pose adorns Morecambe and is a tourist attraction. Footballer Billy Bremner stands guard at his beloved Leeds. So Bolton needs a Fred.' How right she was!

The scheme quickly got under way and an appeals committee was formed. Fred's public loved the idea, they picked up the baton and ran with it and the race was on.

The ambitious plan was to first raise the money (over £40,000) and then commission and erect a bronze statue in time for what would have been Fred's 70th birthday – a tall order, with a timescale of just three and a half years.

Fred at one and a half times size in front of the Hick Hargreaves engine that he helped to save.

In a 2005 ceremony a prestigious Blue Plaque was unveiled on the front of 121 Radcliffe Road, Bolton, Fred's former home. The inscription on the plaque reads: 'Home of the late Dr Fred Dibnah, MBE, steeplejack. Honorary doctorate, Aberdeen and Birmingham universities, artist, draughtsman, carpenter, stone mason, demolition expert, intuitive engineer, steam enthusiast, devotee of our industrial heritage, raconteur and television celebrity. Revered son of Bolton 1938–2004.'

But against all the odds, the race was won. The finishing line was crossed at just after noon on 29 April as the Mayor of Bolton, Coun Barbara Ronson, unveiled the statue.

Prior to the unveiling television producer/director David Hall made a short speech outlining the significance of the location of the statue and fondly recalling the time he had spent with Fred, confirming that the two men became not just media colleagues but good friends. After Brian Tetlow, of the Bolton Civic Trust had thanked his hard working committee members and the local council for their support it was the turn of Fred's widow Sheila to address those gathered to witness the event.

Songwriter Pete Martin led the crowd in a rendition of Happy Birthday followed by his own original tribute song, *Ohh, Ohh Fred Dibnah*.

Mrs Dibnah thanked all who had worked so hard to raise the money which had made the creation of the statue a reality, telling the onlookers that the town centre location was a great choice as the preserved Hick Hargreaves Improved Corliss engine displayed nearby had been one of Fred's favourite restoration projects.

Fred, always a man of the people, now stands proud among his friends in the town he loved. The buzz among the crowd fell to a reverent hush before the cover was whipped off to unveil Fred's smiling face and people jostled to get a look at his bronze, 8ft-tall sculpture, one-and-a-half times Fred's actual size, designed by Jane Robbins. It depicts him in work clothes and trademark flat cap, holding a lightning conductor.

'Did yer like that?' The assembled crowd certainly did. Immediately after the unveiling, songwriter Pete Martin led the crowd in a rendition of Happy Birthday as well as his own original tribute song, *Ohh, Ohh Fred Dibnah*.

Fred stands alongside the encased Hick Hargreaves Corliss stationary steam engine – a historic piece of machinery which he greatly admired and had a hand in saving. Sculptress Jane Robbins was relieved to finally see the statue in place. 'I'm very happy because people have been saying very nice things about it and that's all I wanted – the people of Bolton to like it. I hope people grow to feel that it's theirs, to honour a man that they're very proud of.'

The family were all pleased with the outcome and issued this statement to *Old Glory* on behalf of the children: 'Jayne, Lorna, Caroline, Jack and Roger wish to thank the Civic Trust and The Bolton News for all the effort and work involved in making this happen today, on what would have been our father's birthday. While the main thanks have to go to everyone who donated money to the fund, particular thanks must go to Brian Tetlow (chairman Civic Trust) and especially to Bill Greenhalgh, a friend of dad for over forty years, without whose inspiration this statue would never have come to fruition'.

DR **FRED DIBNAH** M.B.E.

STEEPLEJACK

Honorary Doctorates:
Universities of
Robert Gorton, Aberdeen
5th July 2000
and Birmingham
19th July 2004

REVERED SON OF BOLTON
1938 - 2004

Job done! A proud Bill Greenhalgh on 29 April after seeing the statue of his lifelong friend unveiled.

My brother! It was a proud day for Graham Dibnah when he witnessed the unveiling of a statue to his elder brother, in their home town of Bolton.

Fred Dibnah in pencils, drawn by his friend Bill Greenhalgh.

Fred Said . . .

Did yer like that?

The modern world stinks.

I'm just a bum who climbs chimneys.

A man who says he feels no fear is either a fool or a liar.

One mistake up here, and it's half a day out with the undertaker.

We've become a nation of con-men, living by selling double-glazing to each other.

Height gives you a wonderful feeling of grandeur.

You're the king of the castle up here.

I realise that steam engines aren't everyone's cup of tea, but they're what made England great.

Steam engines don't answer back. You can belt them with a hammer and they say nowt.

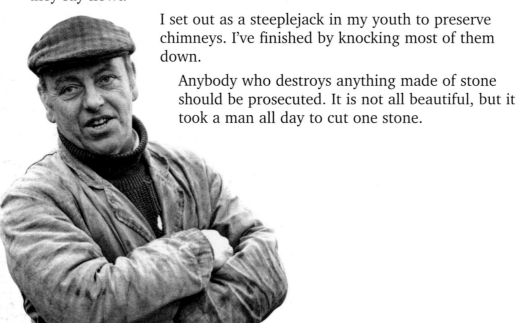

I set out as a steeplejack in my youth to preserve chimneys. I've finished by knocking most of them down.

Anybody who destroys anything made of stone should be prosecuted. It is not all beautiful, but it took a man all day to cut one stone.